Cool Jobs
Ref, Medic, Coach

Written by Abbie Rushton

Illustrated by Jonas Pina

Collins

ref with a coin

soil on boots

ref with a coin

soil on boots

his ear hurts now

the medic runs down

his ear hurts now

the medic runs down

the coach has the gear

the cat gets too near

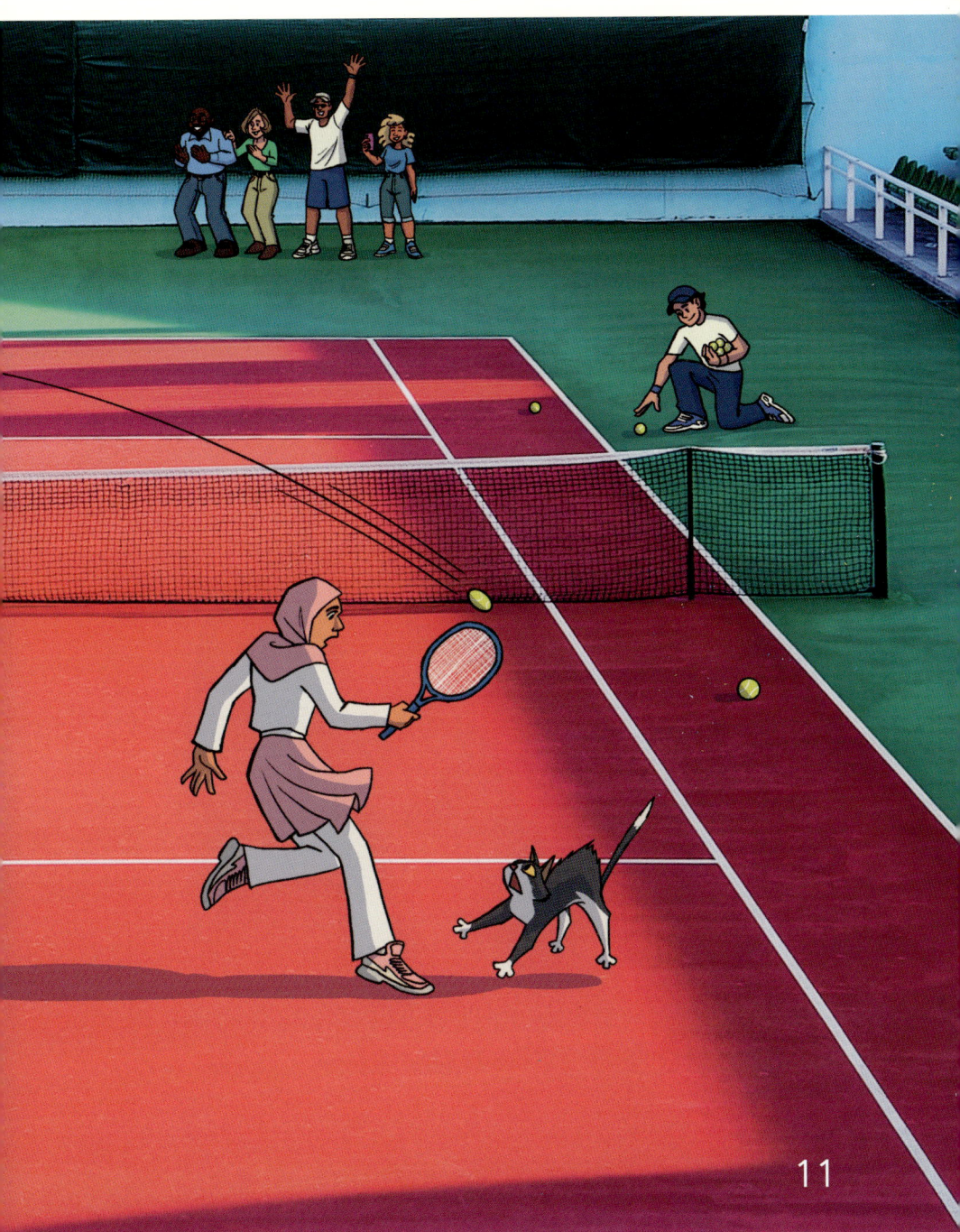

the coach has the gear

the cat gets too near

Review: After reading

Use your assessment from hearing the children read to choose any GPCs, words or tricky words that need additional practice.

Read 1: Decoding
- Use grapheme cards to make any words you need to practise. Model reading those words, using teacher-led blending. Remove the scaffolds as the children become more confident.
- Ask the children to follow as you read the whole book, demonstrating fluency and prosody.

Read 2: Vocabulary
- Look back through the book and discuss the pictures. Encourage the children to talk about details that stand out for them. Use a dialogic talk model to expand on their ideas and recast them in full sentences as naturally as possible.
- Work together to expand vocabulary by naming objects in the pictures that children do not know.
- Discuss the meaning of the words for jobs in sports in this book. Turn to page 2 and say: A **ref** is a shortened name for a referee. Then look at page 7 and discuss how a **medic** is another name for a doctor. Finally on page 10 point to the **coach** and say: A coach is someone who trains athletes, like tennis players.

Read 3: Comprehension
- Ask the children what they already know about the sports and jobs shown in this book. Encourage them to describe their favourite sport and the people who aren't players that help. (e.g. *referee, medic, coach, manager, groundskeeper, camera crew, commentator*)
- Ask: Do you think these jobs are cool? Would you like one of these jobs as a career? Encourage the children to give reasons for their answers.
- Turn to pages 14 and 15. Model using the pictures as prompts to recount the content of the book. Encourage the children to have a go themselves. Use questions for support, such as: What does the referee do? (e.g. *flips a coin*) Who helps anyone who is hurt? (*the medic*) What does the coach do? (e.g. *brings the gear*)